THE TOAD AND THE WATER WITCH

by

ROBERT M. McKINNEY

TALES OF TERRITORIAL
NEW MEXICO

FOR MARIELLE

CONTENTS

PREFACE

Tony Hillerman

Ⓘn those distant days when I was part of *The Santa Fe New Mexican* newsroom crew, putting the Sunday edition to bed was celebrated at a bar just off Burro Alley. There the autopsy was done on the week, victories celebrated and goofups mourned. With that done attention turned to the preoccupation of all newsmen — the effort to understand the publisher.

Most publishers, we believed, were easy to fathom. Robert McKinney wasn't. We knew he had written *Hymn to Wreckage*, A Picaresque Interpretation of History. We knew that well-used language was important to him — a value sadly rare among publishers as a class. (The men and women on McKinney's news staff had shortcomings aplenty, but bad writing wasn't among them.)

But what else did we know about him?

Even when he was away serving as Ambassador to Switzerland, he made detailed analyses of how we covered our territory, of what parts of a reporter's beat were being missed, of which segments of our population were made invisible by lack of coverage. And we also sensed that his interest in the people of *Río Arriba* went much deeper than circulation figures.

The human stories told by the poetry in this little book demonstrate how right we were about that. In them you hear the voice of a most complicated man. I trust you will enjoy them as much as I have.

INTRODUCTION
A WORLD APART

T he old name for upper New Mexico was *Río Arriba*,
Up-River Country. Jokesters called the river *Río Bravo
del Norte*, Wild River of the North. Those who had
never seen water called it *Río Grande*. Barrier mountains
and deserts made this far-away land a world apart, a world
all its own, the littlest.

I first went to the *Río Arriba* when I was ten, ten years
after New Mexico Territory entered the Union. The old
ways of territorial days lingered on through my youth.

Although the Spanish natives were Catholic, Anglo
newcomers were Protestant; all got along well together.
My father was a circuit-riding Protestant preacher who,
when he was not preaching, kept bees. Towing our hives in
a wobbly trailer behind our Ford, we followed the clover
blossoms from one snow-watered meadow to another, a
jump ahead of the hay-mowers. Early and mid-week we
worked with our bees. On Fridays my father thought up
his sermons; on Saturdays he beat the bushes for church-
goers, on Sundays he preached in some friend's parlor,
store, livery stable or cottonwood grove.

Time in the *Río Arriba* followed rhythms and patterns
different from time in the lowlands where we had lived before.
Mornings we drove through hamlets where goats trod grain
from chaff on earthen threshing floors. Noontimes we ate
sardines and crackers beside dripping water wheels. Evenings
we sat by pitch-pine fires while the neighbors — the *gente* —
told each other stories, romantic, comic, tragic and bawdy.

We knew people like those in these tales. The happy-go-lucky Ambrosios; the greedy Domingos. The sensuous, imperious Agapitas. The Josefas who, for the sake of their children, put up with no-good husbands; the parish priests whose every gesture was a sacrament; the cranky debt-ridden storekeepers; the old wagon train bosses and sheep band captains come home in time to die.

Those with no caste and no homes: unkempt children raised with the cows and donkeys; wandering peddlers, fiddlers, toothpullers, knife grinders, stereoptican picture-takers and unattached ladies who travelled from village to village together for company.

I hung out in *tiendas* stocked with calico, flypaper, snuff, plug tobacco, striped candy and pickles, and in livery stables filled with oat sacks, harness and unpatchable inner tubes. I froze in blizzards in sheep camps and sang at tree-felling bees in Christmas snows. I learned that, of all worldly offices, the most awesome job was to be irrigation ditch *mayordomo* in a barren land. I learned why mystics come only from deserts.

I saw what drought, wind and sand; what flood, ice and fire; what murrain and blight could do to those who had no one to help them except San Ysidro Labrador and two in-experienced angels who occasionally, but not very often, ploughed for them while they slept. Still, the *gente* were healthy, happy and sinful. They knew that God lived, lived amongst them, and would forgive any sin except leaving the *Río Arriba*.

Each Lent the farmers would mend their irrigation ditches and hoe the dry clods in their gardens. On Good Fridays, for fear of bad luck, nothing dared stir, even the wind. On Saturdays the wind would scourge the snow from the mountains. On Easter mornings the wind would scour the valleys. Tireless and loud, the wind would mix blossoms with sand and bring Spring. On Good Fridays the *gente* repented their own sins and their neighbor's sins. On Saturdays all sins lay decently buried.

On Easter Sundays came Resurrection. Then the next cycle started. During the twelve months to come a single ambition—*Try to live until Easter*—would unite the *gente*, their flocks, gardens and orchards.

Seasons and ceremonies meant more than calendars. To tell one day from another, people would say, "before the apricots froze," or "before so-and-so's funeral," or "after such and such wedding."

As my father and I drove or rode horseback on high windy ridges we watched churchyard processions below, the *gente* marching with banners, blowing trumpets and firing shotguns. Before Easter, trumpets would mourn, banners would droop, and shotguns would salute the dead. After Easter happy trumpets, banners and shotguns would celebrate weddings.

When the celebrations were over, those who saw no use in hanging onto frail bodies through another dry, hot summer and another long, cold winter could let go without worrying that they would be missed. Then the relatives would gather. The head of the family would lean down and take the tired hand of the one about to depart. He would whisper tenderly the ritual question, *"¿ A dónde vas?"*

A smile and a whisper would come back, *"I go to prepare a place for you."*

This little world apart I lived in before it vanished. My heart never went back to the flat lands.

🍃 🍃

THE TOAD AND THE WATER WITCH

THE TOAD AND THE WATER WITCH

ONE

Bustillo came up from the maize patch
and said to Josefa, "Has the padre
come yet? Where is the old drunkard?"

"Why fret?" said Josefa. "He
always gets here by supper."

"He does not come often to
take his dish at our table.
Be ready. Will our parlor be full
after confession this evening?"

"What else has anyone talked of—
that, and Toribio's wife
keeping the midwife running."

"Her belly is not even full yet."

"She is too small in the hips;
she is too young and too scared.
I tell you, our Pita's too young
for the wicked old Toad."

"Don't you call him *El Sapo*.
He owns half the whole village,
he owns half the whole valley.
Call him Domínguez,
call him *Patrón*, call him *El Rico*,

but call him Old Toad and
we'll never call him our son."

"The Toad's wives die; they all die."

"He only had two, they died
having children—fine children."

"Half as old as our Pita."

"I don't see Pita. Where is she?"

"Watching Ambrosio work on the wagon.
The bolt broke on the singletree."

"The cart's in the shed; Pita's in it;
Ambrosio's in it, inside her.
Keep the girl away from that goat."

"Ambrosio has a fine trade. With
forked willows he dowses for water.
His mother is my mother's cousin."

"Call her. The dowser has teeth:
call the girl and look at her breasts."

TWO

There were paths scorched, white,
where the lean, dark, barefooted men
hurried and skipped through the sandburrs;
paths cool and damp by the water courses
where they walked with great slowness.
There were ways through the bean fields,

4

past sheds roofed with fresh hay.
The ditches smelled of rich silt;
they smelled like hay after cutting.

The padre came down the path,
the barefooted people beside him.
Erect in his pride, Bustillo
moved his bare feet on the earth.
"These are good fields, these fields
that I have here. Now Padre, this
wedding, we'll have it tomorrow!"

"The girl to the Toad for his money?
No priest could ever forgive you."

"The dear children can't wait."

"Who calls Domingo a child?"

"To be *chico*, sleep with *chiquita*."

"Has the Toad slept with the girl?"

"God and I pardon all sleeping.
But, *Reverendo*, you know how
you hate a bride with a melon."

"No banns have even been posted."

"Now, padre. We promise you silver,
enough silver and enough brandy
to make it even feel holy
to bugger a snake on the altar."

THREE

Ahead, where the flume spouted water
on the dripping wheel of his grist mill,
stood Don Domingo Domínguez,
El Sapo — "Old Toad" — to his friends,
admirers, detractors and debtors;
but for his frog eyes and pot-belly,
but for his bow legs and bald head,
the handsomest man in the valley;
wearing a shirt with no collar,
wearing a vest with no buttons;
patrón of ewes beyond number,
owner of cows beyond counting;
lender of money to widows
and forecloser on orphans;
widower of two deceased beauties
whom he never once struck with his stick;
Don Domingo Domínguez, *El Rico,*
waited to greet the procession
and simper and wink at the priest.

FOUR

On ahead, in the shed of Bustillo,
side by side in the bed of the wagon
Ambrosio lay with the daughter,
Ambrosio the long-haired, the laugher,
whistler, flute-carver and singer,
jolly spendthrift, owner of nothing
but his shirt, his trousers and clasp-knife —
the blade honed to whittle with magic
the green wands, twitching and pulling,

water-witches use to discover
sweet hidden streams in the ground —
side by side with young Agapita,
the slender, the small, the high-breasted,
her lips always open but comely,
pouting and full as if bee-stung.

"Domínguez is horrid!" said Pita.
"They can't make me marry *El Sapo*.
I'll run away from the Toad."

"Then your mother will beg in the road
for all the spent money Domingo
has lent her since you were twelve."

"Let him wait until I am older."

"Bustillo knows what we do here.
One slip, and Domingo's a father
before he sleeps with his bride."

"Even if they make me marry,
I won't cook or fetch water
or let him lay in my quilts."

"If he locks you up, can we meet?
Be good, until after the wedding.
I'll think of how to come calling
often on *Patrona* Domínguez.
Perhaps she might need a new well?"

FIVE

Patrón and *Patrona* Domínguez,
home from their bridal trip on the train,
stared at the drowned hogs in their well.

The bride turned up her pert nose
and cuffed her husband's two children.
"Count them yourselves if you want to.
I can't stand the sight or the smell."

"Papa, all eight!" cried Naranja.

"They fell in the night of the
wedding, they've been drowned
for a week!" shouted Bernal.

"One would be chance," said Domingo.
"Two would be fate, even three.
But eight hogs, eight hogs in one well?"

"Your wellhouse is rotten, *El Sapo*.
Watch you don't fall in," said Pita.

The bridegroom wheeled and turned purple.
"Call me husband, call me Domínguez,
call me anything, even old fool,
but in front of both of my children
don't ever call me Old Toad.
Do I want my bone and my blood
cheeping 'Old Toad' at their father?"

"Quit hopping," said the bride sweetly.
She turned and patted the children.

8

"*Queridos,* let's all promise Papa
we'll only say Toad when he hops.
Now *hombre,* fetch a bucket of water."

"In this house, wives haul the water."

Pita slid the pail down the pulley
and hit a drowned hog in the groin.
"We'll live on this till tomorrow,
when Ambrosio can find a new well."

SIX

His sorrows drowned in peach brandy,
El Sapo slept the next morning till
the braying, blowing and drumming
pried up his head from his pallet.
Out on the vine-covered portal
he started to wash in the basin,
then sickened and puked
from the smell of the hog slime.

Round the corner came the procession:
her pigtails braided with blossoms,
her dress pulled up to her haunches,
Pita bounced astride the old burro;
next came Bernal, blowing a trumpet;
then Naranja, beating a dishpan;
last, with a flowering peach branch
came Ambrosio dowsing for water.

Domínguez clouted the children;
he turned on the water-witch, shouting.

9

"God bless your headache, *Sir Sapo*,"
the young wife said with mock solace.

Ambrosio bowed and spoke gently,
"The underground stream is foul from
the hog stink; the channel flows fresh
to the well and putrid beyond it.
The flowering peach wand will show
where hid waters run in the earth."

"I'll do my own water-witching.
I'll dig my own well to clean water."

"Without a dowser to show him
one hits hard rock or caliche."

"That side of the haystack," pointed *Sapo*,
"the lilacs are bluer and bloom first;
their roots reach a rock fissure."
Domínguez stomped off to the house.

"*Patrón*, may sweet water find you,"
Ambrosio called to his shirt tail,
then chucked the bride on the chin.
He fed his branch to the donkey,
walked off and Pita went indoors.
The lorn children stayed by the burro.

SEVEN

In their nest on top of the haystack,
like dragonflies on a flower,
the young wife lazed with the dowser,
their bare skins hot in the sunshine.

10

"Hoist!" came the shout.
"Crack," went the mule whip.
"Screech," went the wheel in the pulley.
  Pita tunneled the hay; looked down
  on the lilacs, down at the tripod
  over the well shaft, at the fresh dirt
  piled up beside it, at the children
  coaxing the burro, at the bucket
  climbing slow up the pulley.

"Whoa!" Naranja cried to the donkey.
  Bernal dumped out the bucket.
  Ambrosio crept to the peephole,
  his hand on Pita's fair shoulder.

"He's struck rock!" said Bernal, "I see
  sparks in the dark and hear cursing."
  Then Sapo's hat — his peaked hat
  which he never took off in his baldness —
  rose from the shaft, up the ladder.

  He climbed out and took off his jumper.
"No more dirt, not even a spoonful.
  Now for the drill and the dynamite."

"Papa, you'll blow us all up,"
  wept his daughter. "If there's rock,
  how can you find any water?"

"The rock's cracked; there's a trickle.
  We've nearly struck it. We'll show them!"
  He slapped his leg, patted the children,
  he fed dried plums to the burro.

In their nest on top of the haystack,
the two rubbed each other with butter
and lay back to doze in the sun.

EIGHT

Domínguez peered down the well shaft.
Aiming the sharp drills, he speared
the bull's-eye of light at the bottom.
He filled his pockets with matches,
he stuffed his jumper with fuses.
Wrapping each stick in a gunny sack,
he packed the bucket with dynamite.
"Bernal, look out! Naranja, stand back!"
Then he lowered the bucket as gently
as if on a line he were drifting
a worm to a fast-asleep fish.

The Toad stroked the mouse-colored burro;
to calm and gentle the donkey, he
lifted its tail and scratched with a twig
the soft hairless skin at the root.
Then, as if his life were hung on it,
he buckled each strap of the harness.

From the step at the top of the ladder,
he went over the plan with the children.
"As soon as I light the fuses,
Hoist me to the top in a hurry.
I mount in the bucket, not by the ladder.
When I step in the bucket I'll holler.
I'll holler and jiggle the well rope.
Six blasts shoot off at once.

Watch. It may take hours, but watch!
Look and breathe with your ears!"

"Naranja, hang onto the halter.
Bernal, hold tight to the mule whip.
When the rope shakes, whack him.
Snap the popper clean off the whip,
then whip the butt off the burro.
We'll be in the house eating plums
when the boom goes off from the blast."
El Sapo sank back down the well shaft.

On the haystack, stretched beside Pita,
Ambrosio tapped with his fingers
the bumps on her spine, blew in her ear;
he stroked the swales of her haunches.
Pita drove a kick to his belly,
then lifted his head to the peephole.
They stared at the jittering children,
at the burro shrugging off flies
and the dark mouth of the well.

NINE

To a humming of bees in the lilacs,
to a cooing of doves in the shed,
to a buzzing of flies in the milk-house,
to the sound of hoppers and crickets,
the waves of the day mounted higher
and drowned the village in noon.

Combing the burrs from her mongrel,
Naranja popped fleas with her nails.

13

Bernal dug worms from the earth
and cut them, squirming, in sections;
he pulled the legs off of ants.

Scratching its rump on the tripod,
the burro hooked his trace on a pole.

"Ho, *hola!*" came the shout from the well.
"I lit the fuses. Haul up, haul up!"

Untangling the trace from the pole tip
Bernal slashed a welt on the donkey.

The pulley swung wild on the tripod.
The pulley-block groaned from the burden,
the donkey sagged from the strain,
then laid its ears back and halted;
balked; bit and kicked at its goaders
who whipped and jerked at its head.

Above the sputtering fuses
hung the beginner at blasting,
swinging, shouting his head off.

The blast rolled through the valley.
Like a buzzard soaring on air drafts
the Toad's hat rose from the shaft,
then the blue jumper, then dust,
then a volley of pebbles,
a shower of water and,
for a moment, a rainbow.

Bernal jabbed his knife in the burro
just as the boom hit the surface.
The scared donkey lit on the cur
that buried her fangs in his belly.

Hitched to the harness, the well-rope
whirred and sang on the pulley.

The bucket bent tight to his feet,
El Sapo shot up with the roar;
then burro, tripod and Domingo
went bumping off in the brush.

Ambrosio jumped in his trousers.
Agapita pulled on his shirt.
They slid from the haystack.
Hopping barefoot through cactus,
opening his knifeblade on the run,
Ambrosio cried out in pity,
"I'll cut you loose! Here we come!"
Agapita grabbed up the mule whip,
whacked at the head of her lover
and slashed at the burro in fury.

"Save me!" cried Domingo in anguish.

"Will you keep out of my bed forever?
Can Ambrosio move in, instead?"

Only groans came from the husband.
She slashed the whip at his face.
"We'll drag you, haul you and pull you,
Then dump you back in the well."

15

"I'll do it," moaned Domingo. "I'll do it."

Ambrosio cut the trace from the harness,
forced open the sides of the bucket
and pried the Toad's feet from the pail.
The burro lit out for the hills.

Gently the two lifted *El Sapo*
and carried him into the parlor.
They took off his shirt and torn trousers,
washed Domingo's bruises and cuts
and pulled the thorns from his hide.
They laid a cool rag on his forehead;
they drew the curtains to rest him.

The cricket that lived in the parlor
dug deeper his hole in the floor.
Only dust moved in the quiet.
Chilled, Agapita shivered.
The shirt slipped from her shoulders;
Ambrosio took her in his arms.

TEN

One windy Spring evening, long after,
buggywheels crunched in the drive
to the Toad family homeplace.
The *Patrona* put her whip in the socket,
jumped to the ground from her journey —
collecting the rents and the interest,
shares from the calves and the sheep-clip —
down lanes lined with bushes in blossom,
by ditches ice-tunneled and snow-banked.

The door to the parlor swung open;
inside her parents and uncles,
her aunts and poor distant cousins,
simple, lazy and pleasant, all cringers
and fawners on the house of El Rico,
waited to pay their monthly respects.
Pita had coins and smiles for them all.

She went from the house to the portal,
to the log bench by the wellhouse
where Sapo sat smoking and laughing,
Ambrosio whistling and joking.
The Patrona kissed both her dear men—
only one of them frog-eyed and bow-legged;
both bald, with handsome pot-bellies.

She waved to the yardful of children,
laughing, chasing, catching, spearing
petals of plums on thorns of the rose.

ELEVEN

You plums which ripen in Summer;
you plums which shrivel and dry;
you plums, bird-eaten and sung-to;
you petals of plums in the Spring!

You Spring, wind-swept and ugly;
Springtime, dry, cruel and bare;
Spring, when the heartbroken
die with exquisite delight!

You tumbleweeds on the crosses;
you roads to bare cemeteries
where colts and calves in their frisking
trample new petals and dung!

You processions with coffins, with banners
which lean in the wind toward the dead;
you children whose dear ribboned hats
blow off and roll in the graves!

You plums! After awhile you ripen;
you are small, hardly much darker
than the last pink-speckled buds.

All day and all night for a summer
the wild brown bees carry honey
from yellow sage and blue clover
to holes in trunks of dead trees.
The wind stores more in you plums.

NEARER TAOS THAN HERE

NO SUCH PLACE

❧

On the far side of the Sangre de Cristos, between the meadows toward the mountains and the sagebrush toward the Rio Grande, is Taos—*if it is anywhere at all.* One is not certain.

The narrow gauge railway runs on the far side of the gorge and meets the stage at a train stop some call Taos, but this is not Taos. It is only Taos Junction, cursed with the name *Stong* in the railway timetable.

In a weed-filled plaza on the road from Peñasco, mud buttresses prop a sagging church. Is this Taos? It is only Ranchos de Taos.

By the stony creek from the mountains, among the hay-fields where the bees live, are corrals, barns and maize patches. The people wear white cotton blankets, they climb from roomtop to housetop on ladders. Is this Taos? It is only the Indian pueblo.

On the road from Questa, another town around a square lined with cottonwood trees and hitching rails. The houses have white pillared porches and sky-blue casements; some houses have acetylene lamps. Behind garden walls irrigation ditches sparkle in the sunshine. Is this Taos? It is only the Anglo town, least Taos of them all.

Taos is a poor devil of a sheepherder's idea of the great world and the great world's idea of the little lost world of the Sangre de Cristos. It is elementary both that there can be no such place and that there has to be such a place.

One says, *"I have come from Taos,"* or *"I am going to Taos,"* but never, *"I am here."*

❧ ❧

JOHN GAME LEG

*In each inaccessible valley the storekeeper was the only one
with any money, consequently any authority. In one valley
where strangers seldom came lived an old German storekeeper with a twisted leg. Trying to balance what his
valley bought outside with what it sold kept him bitter,
as did his crippled leg and his sorrow that his children
were not his own.*

Abel:
"John Game Leg's wife will
not live through another.
Last night he smashed
a table top on her."

Pérez:
"This morning he turned his dog
in on Jesus Menéndez' sheep.
The blind beggar from Piedras
he knocked down with his buggy."

Abran:
"The winter still is not over.
There is no one who does
not owe him money.

"Come with me to Otero's;
I have to take back his adze
and his axe before dinner."

Flavio:
"Abrán! Don't go yet, Abrán!
The men are all at the store.
John Game Leg has something to say."

John Game Leg:
"This town must have money.
I will not sell coffee,
I will not sell flour.
You will have no coal oil
for the lanterns, no shears
when it's time for the sheep clip."

    Abel:
    "It has been winter since summer —
    a hot dry summer, then ice.
    When you bought the sheep clip,
    you said, 'Wool is not dear.
    I cannot pay much.'"

Abrán:
"The corn was poor in our gardens.
All winter we have bought meal."

    John Game Leg:
    "This valley must have money.
    Nothing works without money.
    I will send half the men south
    to lay track on the railroad.
    I will say to the cacique in Seco
    'Here are dirt diggers to dig

the ditch up the cliff to the Hondo.'
"If you cannot pay, I will nail
the door shut. Stay out!
Must I feed the whole valley through
Winter then through the Spring?"

John Game Leg put on his hat.
From the dust of the plaza
he turned and called back:
"All men must leave and get work,
even old men, boys over twelve,
old women, too. Only girls and
young women will stay here . . .
children . . . and Estrella the whore."

He shook his stick at the men;
he turned and limped off.

Flavio:
"I could sell the two cows again
if I had not already sold them."

Pérez:
"Who will grow beans or herd sheep
if we all work on the railroad?"

Abrán:
"He snorts and paws like a bull
with a goad broke in his back."

Abel:
"Praxedes! I can hit with
a knife from ten paces.

24

Strike one match to the store
and I kill you from here."

   Abrán:
   "Run, stop Señor Game Leg!"

 Abel:
"Let each man hitch up his wagon;
fill each wagon bed with rocks.
Everyone crowd around Game Leg,
Don't let him go from the square.

"Hurry, load rocks on the wagons.
 Kick his good leg out from under.
 Let them race round the square.
 Whoever mashes him first
 gets first pick in the store."

   Abrán:
   "Go get his wife and Estrella;
    someone must clean up the square."

WHO HAS SEEN THE MOUNTAINS?

If Seferino could have kept
even one shack and a pasture
we would not have come to the plains,
but what would there be in Trampas
except to hunt work? They would say,
"Ha, see the Rivera girls!
They are help in other houses.
It is not like it used to be."
Even Fermín did not stay. He went
to San Jon; I think he is dead.

In this garden things will not grow.
If they grow, they have no taste.
In Trampas the water goes downstream
with a loud sound among the rocks
then climbs from the flume to the gardens.
It is still cold and you cannot think
how straight it makes the stalks grow.
The water here has not even
seen snow; its taste is too sweet.

And how long are the days here!
Long after the light should be gone
the day hangs on like a beggar;
it does not go behind the mountains
with a rush. I have not been past
the mountains where the sun sets
but here, this is the place where the sun
rises when you are in Trampas.
And this is no great place.

It is impossible to see the mountains.
In the Summer the air waves.
In the Fall there is haze across
the draws and, in the Winter, rain.
But now, in the Spring, my heart
breaks itself because the air is clear
and I still cannot see the mountains.
Three ranges lie between us and Trampas.
No one here knows where it is.

Who has seen the mountains?

NO NUÑEZ BELLIDO

Nude, with a cigarillo,
on the edge of the bedstead
sat the slender, small-teated whore.

"*De nada.* You are gracious.
Welcome, whenever you wish.
But marry you? Never.
Yes, I do like you—as much
as I can like your kind.
But is this all you are:

  "*'Your mother, a Nuñez Bellido;*
    you are young but own your own sheep;
    your father, a ditch mayordomo;
    two brothers are going for priest?'"

"It is false, you are all false.
You waste your lives pretending.
Sit naked, sit still, say nothing.
Whores are whores, without any airs."

ORTEGA'S TAVERN

*Just before Easter, Penitentes choose a
man to be Jesus. If he is well crucified, his
health is not helped.*

ONE

"Ho, Esteban, ho! See us at
Orgeta's Tavern tonight."

"Ortega's?"

"After supper, after watering time."

"It is too close to town.
It is too near the houses.
He must not know where we meet."

"Nobody will be passing.
You forget the ditch meeting."

"After supper, after dark."

"Hé, Carlos."

"I know, I know.
Am I an ass? Quit screaming."

"But it is changed.
It is changed: Ortega's."

"I was not told. No one told me."

"It is a better place."

"Miguel, Miguel!"

"Keep shouting and we will
change the place. Keep quiet.
He must not know where we meet."

TWO

"Is everyone here? Who is not here?"

"Here? We are tired waiting."

"It is too dark."

"Light the lights. Light some more lights."

"Ortega!"

"Well, what do you think?"

"There is no use thinking."

"This time there is no use
thinking or talking. He is the man."

"There is nothing he has not done.
If he has not done it,
he is thinking about it."

30

"He used to say, 'There is
a little something in it
for all of us.'"

"He schemed.
He got all Navarro's water.
I was thinking about it."

"I thought you were the one.
You cut in. I nearly had Navarro."

"Quit throwing things.
This is Ortega's house."

"He cleaned Cortez out."

"Cortez owed everybody, but
He cleaned Cortez out to himself."

"Why is not Cortez here?"

"Cortez is not here either;
Cortez was not told."

"Who knows what he guesses?"

"Sunday he told me, 'Well, I guess
we ought to be getting together.
It is about time.' But I said,
'It is for you to say, you set the time'
And he said, 'Why not Ash Wednesday?'"

"Well. We will do it the usual way.
We will begin by saying, 'He is a fine man.
He is good. Look, he has been good.'
Then we will meet before the people and ask,
'Who has been good? Who shall we crucify?
Who will we crucify this year?'
And he will be the one.
We will need a good man.
This year has been a hard year."

"Who has watched the moon?
When is Good Friday?"

"It will be a droll thing.
We will ask him tomorrow."

"Before we start something, let's
grab the meadow in the Hondo.
He has called in his herders to help."

"There may be a few hurt."

"Well?"

"La Cabrona has a load of new girls."

"Ortega!"

FRAY DIEGO'S
BOOK OF HOURS

PAST TSANKAWI

No one is fond of the place,
Neither Spanish nor Indians.
You go through the piñon and juniper;
you find the draw and go up it
to a high clearing, stone walls,
a floor blown clean by the wind.
Cut from live rock in the middle
two stone lions squat for a pounce.

No one ever lived there.
Sometimes, led by a coyote,
though only at sunrise or sunset,
I have seen bowls set before them,
stone bowls with fresh milk and cheese.

PLUM CLOUDS

The color of plum branches is hard
to describe. The bark is roan,
the blossoms break out in the wind.
The sunlight is cool —
like mirrors of sunlight
shone on mud walls by the water.

The people go about with mattocks;
they hoe at the tree trunks.
They find the clods moist, of a smell
as good as the plum blossoms.
It is Spring, but no leaves yet
and plum clouds pink in the wind
at the foot of roan mesas.

THE NO BRIDGE

Where Villita is, is no bridge
but you no more need a bridge
than Old Doña Álvarez
needs bars on her windows.

Wild River of the North—what a joke!
It goes like ewes before lambing.

Uncle Leon rides toward the ford
but falls asleep on his donkey;
when his feet drag in the water
he wakes up with eyes all a-twinkle.

Escudero wants to have streets;
he says they have streets in cities.
But the land-hoers laugh.
Who could make streets today
to walk on tomorrow?
Who knows where he might
want to walk to next morning?

RÍO BRAVO

Happy the wagon-train master
who has made rich crossings
of prairie and desert
and come home to his village
beyond the Wild River,
wiser but still feeling young,
to finish out his years
in the breast of his family.

O, to see the smoke rise
and smell the fat bacon
from each chimney and rooftop
I played on in childhood.
More to me are these rafters,
these walls plastered with mica,
these hide-covered windows,
these soft springy floors, red
and tough from the steer's blood,
than the tiles and fountains
of the Valley of Mexico.

Happy the man who can start
his old age with the same friends
he started his boyhood.

Can I forget the bees
and vines of Chihuahua or
Imelda of the shadowy hair?
Still, at this time and this distance,
I choke to remember.

She still lives with the sutler;
take word of me when you go there.

O, the cold floor of this bedroom!
My dead wife's dead mirror—
my feet bleed from its shards.

The stars crawl, the moon creeps
but night does not start.
When a man quits work, can he sleep?

Past ruts staked with their bones,
on the plains the antelope leap.
Rain plumes frisk slowly after.
On the wet wind, the scent
of the wolves . . . Is it better
to be a stink in a graveyard
or a clean white bone by the trail?

Happy the man whom one night
in his old home does not frighten—
who can wait to say
goodbye in the morning.

*

c.f. Joachim du Bellay (1559), *Heureux qui comme Ulysse a fait un beau voyage.*

SHIPAPU

Evaristo:
Shipapu? Shipapu?
Where did you hear of it?
I am not young, but even
I have not heard of it more
than two or three times.

Batista:
Faugh! Old Shano is mad.
We will follow and shoot him.
We were crazy to use him
when we knew the Indian was mad.

Vargas:
Well, there I was,
riding out past the mesa
to see how old Shano
was herding the sheep
and if he had grub.
The sheep had wandered loose since
he bunched the last bunch.
By a dung fire by a dry bush
he stared up the valley.

Batista:
How hard did you beat him?

Vargas:
I tied my horse. I walked up
but he did not move.

I sat on a stone.
He kept staring so I thought
"Well, he may see something.
I will wait." It was cold
so I kept the fire going.
He stared until dusk, until dark,
until all the stars had climbed
from the world down below.

Then, at last, old Shano stood up.
He started to roll up his bedroll.

He saw me and took off his peaked hat.
"I did not see you, *patrón*," he said,
"I am going to Shipapu." He called
his dog and walked off in the dark.

Batista:
We will follow and shoot him.

Evaristo:
The Indians, before they came here,
had to live somewhere. They climbed
from the world down below
where they lived with their gods —
tall gods made of lightning and hail.
They climbed through a hole.
The name of their world
is forgot, but old Indians
know where the hole is.
It is secret; instead of its
real name they say Shipapu.

Vargas:
Our saints are sniveling women,
our men have turned into girls.
After what we have done to the Indians,
who can help us if their gods climb here?

     Batista:
     Let us follow and shoot him.

HO, MARIO!

Mario, the lost sheep herder,
bunched his flock for the last time.
He slit a downed ewe; he sucked
the blood from her throat.
His eyes burned; his head swam.
He heard voices from childhood:

"Are you ever coming home again?"

Mario raised up. The sheep stirred
in the thicket. "Who cried?"
The valleys crack empty,
the iron mesas rust.
"Mother, mother, the grass burns!
The sick sheep cannot eat it."

"Are you never coming home? Mario!"

"Who knows? Each day, another league
turns to sand between my fingers.
The rams think they smell water
But can they if I, who remember
the pools, am faint? Pools, pools,
and you quicksands, see my face!"

Ho! Mario!

LÓPEZ WENT

"Tell me the name of the man
who has been out of this valley."

"López went. López went."

"I do not know López.
You make fun.
No one is named López."

"López went."

"If López went, no one went."

"López went."

"López?"

"Even before the river
ran over López went."

"The river never ran over."

"Once was it full but even
before that López went."

"López."

"Wherever he is he is dead.
If he had stayed here
López would be dead."

41

"I know no one named López."

"If he had stayed here
he would be dead."

"How did he go?"

"I do not know. No one knows.
He did not come back."

"He must have gone over the mountains."

"He must have gone over the
mountains."

"The river hardly even runs.
It never runs all summer.
If López went, I am going."

"You would not find him. You might
not even find the way back."

"Who knows if one even looks for
the way back when he has gone?
When López looked at the mountains
Which way did he look?"

"He was the one. López.
No one remembers López."

"All the ground here is ploughed.
It is ploughed, then it blows.
The mountains are not ploughed."

"Only hunters go there.
If they cannot come down
at nights they build fires."

"It may be that what lies beyond
the mountains are more mountains.
It may only be deserts."

"No one knows for sure."

"I know."

"What?"

"I do not know."

PAULA IN SANTA FE

I did not know Padre Diego was dead.
When the sisters read what you sent
they took both my hands and they wept.
They said Padre Diego was dead.

He was nearly a saint.
I did not think he could die.

Even at noon it is dark
where I kneel when I pray
to go back to del Norte.
The town is asleep then like
an old dog in the sun.

Vences has pulled down the blinds
in his store and he snores.

The field hands have not gone back
to the fields. Even the shepherds
have pulled their peaked hats
down over their eyes. But Padre
Diego is dead; all that is ended.

Here at evening they ring the bell
in the chapel; the cathedral bell
over by the square rings. But, when
these have stopped, you can hear,
far away, other church bells,
faint, like cow bells when the cows at
home go down to the river

when it is growing towards night.
The bells go fainter and fainter
until the last cow is standing
watching the drops from her muzzle
ripple on the still, shining water.

O Juan, why be a nun in a convent
when the only saint we can know
is now dead?

SO DO THE SUN AND MOON

Juan Madero who, though he was young,
was a good sheep herder,
waited for them to bring his supper.
The sun went down. It got dark
and then cool, but no one came.

"O ho," he said. "If they do not
bring supper, I must sing for it."
He sang. He sang until he was hungry.

    Little Luisa came up in the dark
    with the cheese and milk.
    "I did not want to come up
    while you were singing," she said,
    "but here it is."

"Ha," he said, "give me the cheese and milk.
I will sing after supper. I am starved."

    "We were all late."

"Has something happened?"

    "Just before suppertime a cart passed
    selling trinkets. Everyone came."

"Did you bring me anything?"

    "Well, if you will make a bark pipe,
    I will tie a ribbon on it."

"I have finished. You are the one
  who was late. You do the singing."

    "Did anyone ever know the names
      of all the stars, Juan?"

"They have no names,
  or else they are named wrong.
  No one knows their names."

    "Everything has a name."

"The branch of stars above the trees
  they call the Rain Stars.
  There are six Rain Stars
  but they do not bring the rain
  nor do Indians beating the drums.
  It is Madre María."

    "Many stars are named," said Luisa.

"I cannot see the shapes
  they say they resemble.
  They rise and go across the sky
  but I do not know their names."

    "They travel. They travel all the time."

"But when they have made one path
  they go a little to the side, until
  like sheep beating paths on the hill,
  soon they go through the whole sky."

47

"So do the sun and the moon."

"The shooting stars cry their cry
while they hurry.
They cry and it rings about them;
they cannot hear the others.
They go in a hurry, but they see
the same country. And what is time?
A man on horseback cannot see everything."

"Every night is different
from another," said Luisa.

"When I was a boy and watched the sheep
I thought that each saint had a chance
to make one night like he wanted.
He had the clouds sent or used the moon,
or decided only to have the stars brighter.
I tried to guess what saint it was
from the kind of night it was,
and I decided that all the saints,
at least in this country, were men."

"Who decided on this night?"

"Each star is a trumpet,
I would say San Gabriel made it."

"You are funny, Juan. That is papa calling."

EUSTALIA'S WELL

Cristóbal:
How can I say what I feel?
I speak but say it so poorly.
I feel it, but all by myself.
When I say it, it is not
what I felt all alone;
it turns to what everyone
is shouting out loud.

Ramona:
What have you felt, Cristóbal?

Cristóbal:
That this is the time when it rains,
when it rains and the trees have flowers;
when I run through the creek
twice to you every evening.
I have already quit thinking
about the time before I grew up.
How could anyone say it?
To speak is to shear sheep —
you get only burrs and some wool,
but who could wear a bare sheep?

Ramona:
What have you felt, Cristóbal?

Cristóbal:
The fish in the stream by the willows
do not think of the top of the water;

each time they leap they are caught.
There are ten ways to say what I feel —
but, when I speak, it works backward.
I could never have said something
else. It would be better
if I had kept quiet.

Ramona:
It is not what one says, but
who says it. Do you love me?

Cristóbal:
Yes, I think so. I know that I do,
but how can you tell? I could go
on my knees clear to Chimayó,
but still you might wonder.
One cannot tell how he loves.

Ramona:
Where the sun rises, who knows?
But it always comes up.
That it comes up is enough.

Cristóbal:
Do you remember Eustalia?
She would not believe Rupe loved her;
Rupe drowned himself in the well.

Ramona:
At least, it was her well.

LITTLE THIEF

Mona

Ramón, little Ramón, the plumbush whip!

Ramón

Ho, ho, I do not have to go to bed yet.
See, it is not dark. I can still see.
I am not going far. Only to the woods.

Mona

Into the house, little thief.
Whoever heard of letting a child
run loose in the dark?

Ramón

I am not afraid. I am not afraid
of the dark. I was in the woods
and on the mountains today.

Mona

Mountains change when the sun
goes down. No one goes there.

Ramón

What is wrong with the mountains?

Mona

Before dark they drive the sheep down
from the mountains, and the belled cattle.
The burros are shut in corrals.
Woodcutters build fires in a clearing.

51

Ramón
What is wrong with the mountains?

Mona
The coyotes come out of the shadows;
they run to a clearing; they look
behind before they start yelping.

Ramón
They are afraid. What is wrong?

Mona
The deer's hearts pound in the dark.
The dogs hang close to the house.
If a child is lost in the mountains
all day they hunt through the woods,
all night they call on the mountain sides.
They call, *"Ramón, Ramón!"*
Even the coyotes stop yelping.

From the valley you
see the torches;
you hear the men calling.
But, if you tried in the morning
to find the way they have gone,
you could not find a footprint.

Ramón
Mona, it is dark.

CRITICS' COMMENTS

"Something of the Universal"
by Arthur McAnally

This is an extraordinary range of poems. You have caught something of the universal in mankind in the very poetry of the native New Mexican's life. You must indeed know them well. And poetry is such a careful and precise medium for catching the essence. They may lack the customary adornment of fancy, but they certainly are essences of life and emotion and thought. With these who needs bric-a-brac?

Sometimes I think the dramatic poems are best, again I find the others more appealing. *The Toad and The Water Witch* is the best of the dramatic ones. But then *John Game Leg* has the despair and build-up to crisis of tragedy which Samuel Johnson thought was nobler. *Ortega's Tavern* I enjoyed also, not only for the matter-of-fact facing up to a very great drama of life but also for the humanity of it.

You do catch and portray an emotion well, in *Who Has Seen the Mountains*—I was homesick for New Mexico for several years after I left, and you express so well what I felt vaguely and could never pin down. The *No Bridge* I liked too—it seems to embody an essential truth about our modern complex civilization; it tickles me that you have caught the New Mexico spirit so beautifully.

The poems, *Nearer Taos Than Here*, are very good indeed. They have caught beautifully some of the essential qualities of man, reflect keen insight and understanding, are a pleasure to read, and are in an uncommon poetic style

53

which our society should appreciate if indeed it still can appreciate any poetry at all. The introductory essay is excellent. There would be room for a few more poems if but this is enough as it stands. Congratulations!

Love Poems to the Past
by Paul G. Ruggiers

McKinney is more inclined towards the long narrative form than to the short forms of poetry. His gift is for the longer prose line rather than pure lyric. And his poems are aided greatly by the theory of history and change with which he prefaced his first volume, *Hymn to Wreckage.*

He has none of the elliptical and compressed style of the born lyricist. He has an almost totally unadorned style, without the usual ornaments of rhetorical and poetical figures, all of which poets habitually use. He makes most of his effects by the use of terms for objects with which we have sympathetic associations. . . . So much of what he describes, one has seen over and over again and found in its own way wonderfully pleasant and free from the clutter of modern life. In a way these poems are love poems to the past, evocative commemorations of the simplicity and essential sanity of life.

The Toad and The Water Witch seems to me a work of great competence and great compression. . . . That poem alone is worth the whole volume. . . . If McKinney could do a series of poems like this he would make a great contribution to New Mexico regional art. The poems have somewhat the air of Robert Frost translated into a New Mexico locale with psychological statements about people in remote areas.

The poems are a tremendous burst forward in lyrical impulse, degree of passion and the ability to handle both the characters and the long form itself. In this set of poems McKinney has made a contribution to New Mexico literature.

One thousand copies of this book have been printed
for the friends of Marielle & Robert McKinney
and *The Santa Fe New Mexican.*

🍃

Set in ITC Golden type and printed by letterpress
at The Stinehour Press in Lunenburg, Vermont.

🍃

Press of *The New Mexican*

202 EAST MARCY STREET

SANTA FE, N. M. 87504-1705